AF338134

The Role Families Play in Roman Culture and Society

Ancient History Sourcebook

Children's Ancient History

For the ancient Romans, the most important elements in society were family, household and clan. Let's look at what family life was like in the Roman Empire

For the Romans as for us, the basic family unit was mom, dad and the kids. In the days of the Roman Empire, that family unit was less important. What was important was your extended family—you in relation not just to your parents and brothers and sisters, but to your uncles and aunts, grandparents, cousins and others who in some way counted as part of your "family".

People did not usually marry for love in ancient Rome. The head of the family would start arranging a marriage for the children when they were as young as 14. Husbands were usually several years older than their wives. The point of marriages was to connect families and households to each other, to gain land or wealth (the family of the woman had to provide a "dowry", or payment, to the man's family), and to provide more children to help Rome grow.

Having sons was very important, because the life of the family, the household and the clan depended on sons. If a family had no sons, they would adopt a male child and raise him as a possible future head of the family.

Typically, many family units lived together under one roof in an extended family. Even rich families lived this way, so a household that lived by itself, without other family members nearby or even in the next room, was considered a little deprived.

THE HOUSEHOLD

The Roman household family was a large grouping of many couples. Their children, uncles and aunts, cousins, and more distant family members were all under the leadership of the father of the family (the paterfamilias) and all living under one roof. A wealthy family would also have slaves and servants, and would count them as part of the family and household.

PATERFAMILIAS

The head of the family was almost always the oldest male relative, the father, father-in-law, or grandfather of almost everyone in the house. A grown man, even a general or a senator, was not considered the head of his family if his father was still alive.

Only the paterfamilias could own most property, which in theory he managed for the good of the whole family. Only he could sign a binding contract. Only his word was taken as testimony in a court of law. The grown children of the household did not even have money of their own! All income came to the household, and the paterfamilias gave each male member (or those who deserved it!) an allowance, or peliculum, to spend to support their own family and public life.

'CHARIOTEER'
ROMAN STREET SCENE

The paterfamilias had immense power, both within and beyond the family. He could order people to marry, usually to form bonds with other households, or to divorce. He could declare what children of the household were to be kept, and which could be sold into slavery! He could punish members of the family. At the start of the Roman Republic, before the Empire, the paterfamilias could even have family members put to death.

Nobody in Roman society questioned the authority of the paterfamilias, but some debated how best to use that power. It was agreed that it was perfectly correct to beat a slave who was disobedient or did not do his job well. But some argued that beating your son for disobeying would make him think, and then act, more like a slave than like a Roman citizen. Many of the plays of Terence and Plautus, which were to the Romans as television sit-coms are for us today, included a disobedient son and a father who had to figure out what to do about him without making him slave-like.

You often had a household where the paterfamilias was quite an old man. In the household were his grown children and their families, and their adult children and their families, as well as many other family members. When the paterfamilias died, if he was the last of his generation, the household might split into several households, with each son of the eldest generation becoming (at last!) the paterfamilias of their own household.

MATERFAMILIAS

The senior mother in the household was the materfamilias. As men usually married women who were younger than they were, the materfamilias was often much younger than her husband.

While men had the formal power, in practice, women had a lot of control over the way the household ran, and day-to-day decisions. The materfamilias was in charge of managing the household, directing the servants and slaves, and providing basic education for the children.

For a wealthy or powerful household, the materfamilias also had a role in society. Part of her job was to support her husband's career and ambitions by being a gracious and effective hostess and by making sure she, and the events in the household other people attended, made the paterfamilias look good.

CHILDREN

Life was hard for even the children of wealthy families. Doctors did not understand much about illness and how to keep people healthy, and there were fewer medicines than we have now. About one in four babies died before their first birthday. Half of all children died before reaching age 10.

Families sometimes adopted children from other households to bind the households more closely together. Augustus, the first Roman Emperor, was the adopted son of Julius Caesar, and by that adoption gained status and power.

Augustus

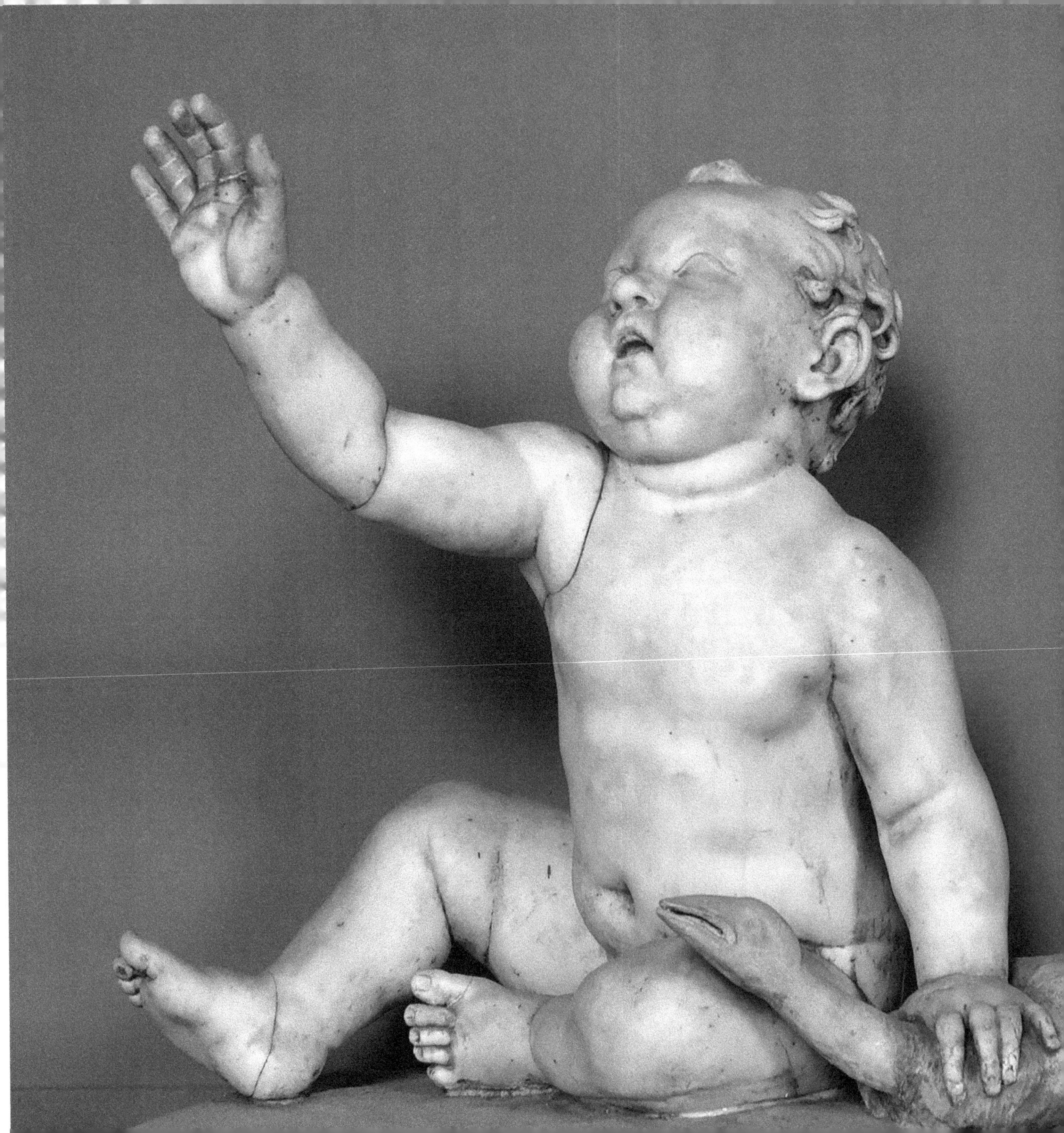

The Empire gave awards to women who had many babies. Once a woman had three babies, she was considered independent and could own property in her own name and start to guide her own life.

Parents did not show love to their children the way parents do now. When a baby was born, the midwife would put the child on the ground in front of the paterfamilias. If he picked the child up, the baby was accepted as part of the family, otherwise, the baby was put out for adoption.

The mother, but probably not the materfamilias, raised both the boys and the girls. Children the family did not want, or could not support, could be sold as slaves.

In the household, the children might help serve the main meal of the day, at the end of the afternoon, but they ate separately. They were not expected to speak to adults or to take part in the main meal.

How much education a child got depended on the situation of the household. There might be a nurse to teach the child Latin and Greek. The father or a slave would teach the boys to swim and ride horses.

When a boy was seven years old, he started learning from a tutor. Students wrote their lessons on wax tablets that they could smooth out and use over and over again, or just wrote in the dirt or sand at their feet. A lot of learning was by memorizing what the tutor told you.

SLAVES

Although slaves were part of the household, they had few or no rights. Many of them were people from other nations who became slaves when Rome conquered those nations in war. Taking slaves was part of Rome's reward for winning!

Many slaves were highly educated, and served as teachers, doctors, architects, and in other skilled trades. Other slaves worked on the country estates of the rich as farmers, or did manual labor.

If slaves managed to gather enough money, they might be able to buy their freedom. A paterfamilias might also convey freedom on a household slave, usually as a reward for long and faithful service.

THE GENS OR CLAN

A clan or gens, was a group of related households A clan usually joined family members, adopted members, and other households of business partners or political allies. In the Roman Republic a few clans, the Gentes Maiores, controlled most political life in Rome.

You took the name of the clan as part of your own name, and the name of your family. For example, if the Scipione household was part of the Fabia clan, and you were of that household, you would be "of the Fabii Scipiones".

When people talk about the Julian or Flavian emperors, they mean the emperors that came from a particular clan. Being part of a clan was not like being in the nobility. Nobility came through holding high and important military and political offices over many generations.

Some clans had special traditions and rituals that were very important. Even when Rome was under attack by tribes from Gaul, the Fabii clan gathered to hold their annual clan ceremony on Rome's Quirinal Hill. In some senses the tie to your clan was stronger than the tie to your country!

Visit

BABY PROFESSOR
EDUCATION KIDS

www.BabyProfessorBooks.com

to download Free Baby Professor eBooks
and view our catalog of new and exciting
Children's Books